D1134556

THREE ASPECTS OF STUART ENGLAND

THE WHIDDEN LECTURES

Series I—January 1956
The Anatomy of South African Misery
C. W. de Kiewiet
President, The University of Rochester

Series II—January 1957
The Evolution of India
Vijaya Lakshmi Pandit
High Commissioner for India to the United Kingdom

Series III—January 1958
Colonial Élites; Rome, Spain and the Americas
Ronald Syme
Camden Professor of Ancient History, University of Oxford

Series IV—January 1959
The Hollow Universe
Charles De Koninck
Professor of the Philosophy of Nature, Laval University

Series V—January 1960
Three Aspects of Stuart England
Sir George Clark
Provost of Oriel College, Oxford, 1947–57

THREE ASPECTS OF STUART ENGLAND

SIR GEORGE CLARK

LONDON
OXFORD UNIVERSITY PRESS
NEW YORK TORONTO
1960

Oxford University Press, Amen House, London E.C.4
GLASGOW NEW YORK TORONTO MELBOURNE WELLINGTON
BOMBAY CALCUTTA MADRAS KARACHI KUALA LUMPUR
CAPE TOWN IBADAN NAIROBI ACCRA

PRINTED IN GREAT BRITAIN

FOREWORD

THE WHIDDEN LECTURES were established in 1954 by E. C. Fox, B.A., LL.D., of Toronto, the senior member of the Board of Governors, to honour the memory of the late Reverend Howard P. Whidden, D.D., LL.D., D.C.L., F.R.S.C., 1871–1952, Chancellor of McMaster University from 1923 to 1941. Their purpose is to help students cross the barriers separating the academic departments of a modern University. The lectures are not restricted as to general theme.

Dr. Whidden was a member of a family resident in Antigonish, N.S., since 1761, after earlier settlement in New England in 1700. Born in Nova Scotia, he was educated at Acadia University, McMaster University, and the University of Chicago, and served as a minister of Baptist churches in Ontario, Manitoba and Ohio. From 1913 to 1923 he was President of Brandon College in Manitoba, then affiliated with McMaster University, and served in the House of Commons in Ottawa from 1917 to 1921 as the Union Government member for Brandon. Assuming executive responsibility at McMaster in 1923, he directed what was for the University practically a second founding, its transfer to Hamilton in 1930, from Toronto where it had been established in 1887. He is remembered as a man of striking appearance, unusual dignity, effective leadership, ready tolerance, deep Christian conviction, and broad educational outlook.

The fifth series of Whidden Lectures were delivered in January 1960, by Sir George Clark, M.A., D.Litt., F.B.A. A master historian and director of historians, whose distinguished career has included the Chichele Professorship of Economic History at Oxford and the Regius Professorship of Modern History at Cambridge, and whose organizing labours are seen in the *Oxford History of England*, *The New Cambridge Modern History* and *The Home University Library*, he is also widely known as a special university lecturer, as in the Creighton Lectures at London, the Ford Lectures at Oxford, the Murray Lectures at Glasgow and the Wiles Lectures at Belfast. His years as Provost of Oriel College have made him also an understanding mentor of undergraduates.

His *Three Aspects of Stuart England* will long be remembered here for his felicitous choice of topic and material, and his effective delivery, and not least for his understanding of the Good Old Cause once dear to the hearts of the ecclesiastical ancestors of the founders of this University. That this was the occasion of his first extended visit to Canada is a further source of gratification to us.

G. P. GILMOUR

PRESIDENT'S OFFICE
McMASTER UNIVERSITY
March 1960

CONTENTS

I

Insularity

MY FIRST WORDS must be to express my very sincere thanks for the invitation to deliver the Whidden Lectures. It has given me the opportunity to enjoy the hospitality of this truly hospitable university, and to offer for your consideration some opinions on the period of history with which my studies have been chiefly concerned. As the first Englishman to be honoured in this way it is perhaps appropriate that I should choose an English subject, and that I should approach it by paying some attention first to the geographical position of Britain. It has long been understood that the position of Britain as an island has a two-sided significance in its history. On the one hand it has served as a protection against attacks and threats of domination from outside, and in its most usual sense the word 'insular' means something like 'inaccessible'. On the other hand, throughout recorded history and in prehistoric times, Britain has been far more accessible to travellers than many continental countries. Geographers explain how its structural slope towards the mainland, the disposition of its ports and rivers, and its internal conformation made it a recipient of peoples and influences from across the Narrow Seas. Then they have shown how, after the great geographical discoveries, set as it is on the world's waterways between the land-masses, it has partaken of the life of all the continents. One geographer summed up this dual insularity as 'in-sulation without isolation'.[1] In this first lecture I shall try to show how this ambiguous insularity defined England's relation to Europe in the Stuart period, that is from the accession of King James I in 1603 to the death of Queen Anne, the last ruler of that house, in 1714.

When I chose Stuart England as the subject of my lectures I did not forget that they were to be delivered in a city founded by George Henry Hamilton, in a University which was originally endowed by Senator William McMaster and bears his name, and in memory of Dr. Whidden, who, though of English descent, was born in Nova Scotia. The reason why I shall have little to say about Scotland or Scotsmen is that, although they had the same sovereign, England and Scotland in the Stuart period were still separate kingdoms. They had close and constant intercourse in many departments of life; considerable parts of their histories belonged equally to both of them; but their institutions and their social structures had developed independently, and it was only in 1707, almost at the end of the period, that the union of the legislatures inaugurated their common political and constitutional history. For the century during which the union was merely personal, Scottish history ran a separate course, at any rate in the matters with which these lectures will deal. The accession of James VI of Scotland to the English throne was, however, a turning-point in the history of British insularity. He was the first king who ever ruled over the whole island, and therefore he was the first to enjoy the strategic security which the surrounding sea conferred, or at least offered at a price.

The consequent change in the geography of English defence had indeed been in a way anticipated during the period of friendly relations before James's accession. Hitherto foreign wars had normally involved two fronts, one, protected by the seas, towards France or the Low Countries, the other open by land towards Scotland. The most northerly part of England had a special organization as a frontier-region, with fortresses on the two coasts, Berwick and Carlisle, which could be supplied by sea, and could serve as bases for operations to the north. Now the special organization of the marches was abolished;[2] the Debatable Lands were debatable no longer, and foreign diplomatists no longer resorted to Edinburgh in search of an ally against England. It is indeed true that a Scottish army crossed the border in 1639, to be followed by others during the two following decades. But their purposes were not interlocked with European affairs by ties like those of the sixteenth century. They resulted from divisions within the Stuart inheritance. They illustrate the general rule that the coalescence of two or more states is usually followed by strains and stresses, partly along the old dividing lines even if partly along new lines which cut across them. And, in spite of all this, the personal union inaugurated the insular strategy.

King James I had no army and he neglected the navy until the last years of his reign. There were always some among his subjects who wanted him to intervene in continental wars, but he succeeded in remaining at peace for the whole five and twenty years. Immediately after his death, his successor Charles I was involved in war first with Spain and then with France as well; but he had no difficulty in disengaging himself from this fruitless fighting. That fighting was indeed one step towards the civil wars of his later years, and these civil wars were European events, of much concern to Spanish, French, Dutch and German statesmen who hoped for British assistance in their own wars, or hoped, by encouraging one side against the other, to keep Britain impotent and out of action. But the civil wars were shut up within the boundaries of the three kingdoms. Charles hired a few German mercenary troops and both sides received shipments of arms from abroad; but no foreign aid made any difference to the character and results of the conflict. If French or Spanish armies had been able to intervene, the revolutionary crisis in Britain might have been many times more severe; but, judging by analogy, it seems much more probable that foreign intervention would have rallied the nation to its own defence. It would have settled its internal quarrels without going to the last extremity. In either case its history would have been fundamentally different.

Soon after the middle of the century, the Dutch built a great fleet and so made it impossible for the

English to enjoy the advantages of insularity without paying the price by the maintenance of a costly navy of their own. Many converging causes brought about a purely maritime war against the Dutch. After that first Dutch war there were two interpretations of the strategy for the island with its navy. The most esteemed poet of the day wrote in 1655:

> Angels and we have this prerogative
> That none can at our happy Seat arrive
> While we descend at pleasure to invade
> The Bad with vengeance and the Good to aid.[3]

Oliver Cromwell said to his parliament in 1658: 'You have accounted yourselves happy in being environed with a great Ditch from all the world beside. Truly you will not be able to keep your Ditch, nor your Shipping,—unless you turn your Ships and Shipping into Troops of Horse and Companies of Foot; and fight to defend yourselves in *terra firma*.'[4] Within six months after that speech a British expeditionary force helped the French to win a victory over the Spaniards outside Dunkirk, but it was many years before the national policy settled firmly into the Cromwellian mould. Throughout the reigns of Charles II and James II, that is through the period of the second and third Dutch wars and through the following period when Britain stood by as a neutral spectator of the aggrandizement of Louis XIV, there was strong opposition to the raising of military forces, and at times there was not even effective support for the maintenance of a navy. As luck would have it no foreign enemy set foot in

England except for a small landing-party which was beaten off from Landguard Fort, outside Harwich, in the second Dutch war. But in 1688 for the first time in just over 200 years, there was a successful landing in force. A near relative of the English royal family landed in the west country, advanced to London and assumed the crown. William III's fleet was Dutch; he came in his personal capacity as sovereign Prince of Orange; his troops were Dutchmen, Danes, French Huguenots and Germans; but this did not count as a foreign invasion. It was an incident of British history. The British navy missed its chance of resisting if it meant to resist, and the British army broke without fighting. Once the expedition had succeeded, the organization of the two British states was put at the disposal of its leader. It was he who finally turned British policy into the direction of sending armies to the continent. From his time until the fall of Napoleon all the British wars against France except one included an expeditionary force acting with continental allies. The command of the sea which made this possible was neither gained immediately nor held without interruptions, but even the war of William III demonstrated that it enabled Great Britain to carry out preparations for war on the largest scale without interference by an enemy.

Although this system of using the island as a base for military operations was the normal policy from that time until our own, there were also normally, or at least very commonly, statesmen who stood for isolation from the continent. In King William's time one of his former ministers provided this opposition with its most famous phrases: 'Look to your Moate. The first Article of an English-man's Political Creed must be, That he believeth in the Sea.'[5] But there was no opposition in the contrary sense. No one wanted to merge England in the continent, to do away with the barrier of the Narrow Seas. Physically that was impossible, but no one even indulged in an idle fancy that the moat should be bridged. Insularity might be used for either of two strategic systems, but in itself it was acknowledged to be an advantage.

There is a contrast between the strategic consequence of insularity, security from hostile invasion, and its consequences in many other departments of life. Communications by water were far cheaper and had a greater carrying-capacity than communications by land. In everything connected with economic life, religion, the arts and the activities of the mind, Britain's insular position rendered her more accessible to influences from abroad than she could have been if the sea had never broken through the Straits of Dover. A considerable part of British economic history in the seventeenth century has been summed up as 'conscious imitation of the Dutch'. Visitors and immigrants of many kinds, from financiers to artisans, brought improvements for English agriculture and business, and so helped to liberate England from her economic dependence on these same Netherlands. That story and the closely related story of the Huguenot refugees have often been told. In the history of English thought and literature foreign influences were equally conspicuous. The scholars and scientists of many universities, amongst which perhaps Padua and Leiden were the chief, stimulated and guided Englishmen by their teaching and their books. As the surviving seventeenth-century libraries in England are explored we are coming to know many details of this intercourse, and also of the foreign gifts to English imaginative literature. We may look forward to having before long complete lists of translations, quotations, and travellers, and to systematic surveys of all the facts; but there is no need of minute investigation to show that French and Italian writers exerted major influences, while Spanish, Portuguese, and others also contributed handsomely, if on a smaller scale. It was not until the last decades of the period that the English began to make a comparable return: Shakespeare, Bacon, Milton, and their contemporaries were little known on the continent in their own time. In the other regions of cultural life, such as music and the visual arts, for one reason and another it was even more the case that England received far more than she imparted.

The state of society was comparatively simple. Each special class of people who desired contact with other countries had its regular means of communication. Travel in western Europe was no longer difficult or hazardous except in theatres of war. Among the leading figures in the seventeenth century there were very few who never went abroad. So far as we know, though some ingenious writers have invented theories to the contrary, Shakespeare never did, nor Oliver Cromwell. Among those who never crossed the Channel or North Sea were Archbishop Laud, John Bunyan, John Dryden, Sir Isaac Newton, Dean Swift and Alexander Pope; but can any equally eminent names be added to this short list? The leaders of English life in the second half of the century were more travelled than those of the first half. For one thing many of them went abroad as exiles during the period of troubles. The grand tour, or shorter tours in France, Germany and the Low Countries, became a common part of education.[6]

Among foreign visitors to England there were very few Frenchmen of the first rank, and that is not surprising if we think of the course of relations with France and of its internal state. Sully, in the first days of James I, came as an ambassador, but none of the greatest French writers ever saw England. With the Low Countries, however, it was different. John of Oldenbarneveld, Hugo Grotius, John de Witt, Christian Huygens, all paid visits. On the whole we must not accept the story that Rembrandt ever saw London;[7] but Rubens did, and van Dyck on his longest visit lived in England for eight years. He was the greatest painter who practised in Stuart England; after the Restoration the leading painters were lesser men, such as the Dutchman Sir Peter Lely, the German Sir Godfrey Kneller and the Swede Michael Dahl. Painting was taking root in England in this time; it had indeed native roots of its own; but on the higher levels it was still almost entirely provided by immigrants. Architecture absorbed elements of several foreign traditions, but, in the nature of the case it was less metropolitan, more widely spread through the country and therefore more home-grown. Music, on the other hand, which had a strong native tradition down to the death of Purcell in 1695, underwent such powerful influences from abroad especially from Germany, that in the early eighteenth century it was dominated by the continent much as painting had been a century earlier. There ceased to be an independent English school.

One after another these foreign influences flowed in, but they came less like a flood spreading on a wide front over empty flats, than like a tide penetrating inland up deep channels to quaysides ready built and equipped. This may be illustrated from the facts of the knowledge of foreign languages among Englishmen of different kinds. At the beginning of the century Latin was still, as it had been for centuries, the medium by which the higher branches of thought and learning were communicated from one country to another. Even within the different countries the vernacular languages did not suffice for the scholar. No modern European language possessed enough books to fit out a comprehensive library of all the sciences. There was not enough demand to bring them into existence. In England mathematicians, theologians, physicians and anatomists did much of their reading and some of their writing in Latin. Bacon wrote his philosophical works in both languages, and Englishmen, like Frenchmen, were extending the use of their own language to more and more of the specialized subjects all through the century. William Harvey published his physiological works in 1628–51 and Newton his *Principia* in 1687, in Latin, but Newton, unlike Harvey, published much in English. The last English book written in Latin which is still widely famous was Heberden's *Commentarii* of 1802: medical research appealed only to a restricted public. The last non-medical book of much note in which an Englishman expressed himself in Latin was perhaps John Woodward's *Naturalis Historia Telluris illustrata et aucta* of 1714: his earlier *Essay towards a Natural History of the Earth* was translated into Latin by the Swiss J. J. Scheuchzer nine years after it appeared in 1695. In 1690 Sir Thomas Pope Blount published a sort of encyclopaedia of literary reputations, *Censura celebriorum Authorum*, and when a second edition appeared at Geneva in 1694 all the quotations in English, French and Italian were translated into Latin.

By a two-sided revolution Latin lost its place as an international language and one by one the vernaculars took over most of its functions. So far as England was concerned the revolution was completed in this period. This did not mean, as some people imagine, that there was a breakdown of international communications, or a weakening of internationalism. For the French indeed there was a new kind of internationalism based on their own language, in diplomacy, in literature and even in conversation over a great part of Europe. For the English all that still lay hidden in a distant future. In the seventeenth century Dutch had more claim to be an international language than English. At least it might with some exaggeration be called a *lingua franca* of the North Sea.[8] But the English did not allow themselves to be isolated by the barrier of language. They participated in the common life of the civilized world to such purpose that, before the end of the Stuart period, British political thought, as well as British institutions, had reached the height from which they soon illuminated the imagination and the endeavour of two continents. For this two linguistic resources were brought into play. First there was more and better language-teaching. Foreign travel as a means of learning languages, I have already mentioned, but the tours of young aristocrats accompanied by tutors were less important in the long run than the more numerous journeys of lesser men. Merchants who learned modern languages and business methods abroad rendered many and varied services. Let me mention two instances at random. Steven Crisp of Colchester, a town which traded with Holland, learned Dutch and German and paid thirteen visits to his fellow-Quakers in Holland.[9] James Houblon, a city man of Huguenot descent, explained a Dutch book on ship-building to Samuel Pepys.[10] There was certainly an increase and an improvement in the formal teaching of French. It formed no part of the curriculum of the universities, but teachers were encouraged to settle in Oxford and Cambridge, and their work was effective.[11]

Teaching was one resource and the other was translation. This is a matter on which research is still in progress. We already have some bibliographies of translations. I would venture the opinion that the supply of English versions of important foreign books became much more adequate, and also that translation itself as an art or science became more scholarly and more serviceable. In accordance with the general tendency of literature at that time it followed the originals more closely. And before leaving the subject of language, I must remind you that this period saw the rise of Oriental studies in England.

In intellectual matters, then, the insular position of England meant that there were many imports, and that soon there was to be much exporting activity. Of course it was not chance that decided what was and what was not imported. In literature and thought there were always contrasts corresponding to the needs of the users. Mathematics, music and painting could be freed from local limitations. Science was completely cosmopolitan. Theology was abstract and applicable to all men alike; but churches were localized and so there was less interest in the details of their government and history except where they were relevant to problems that concerned the English at home. There were divines of the Church of England who had a wide European outlook, and its position beside the other churches especially the Roman and Gallican was discussed copiously. Calvinist and anti-Calvinist sects were aware of their affinities with like-thinking men from Poland

and Hungary to the Netherlands. Broadly speaking, however, in religious matters international currents carried generalized and simplified ideas; there was a residue of the concrete and idiomatic which could not be lifted away from its original soil.[12]

If we turn to social and political institutions we must expect to find the same contrast. We must expect to find foreign influences only when there were needs which the English felt as their neighbours felt them. But was England socially and politically linked with Europe as she was in literature and the arts, or was she isolated as she was strategically? There were only three continental centres which left any noticeable imprint on English institutions. The first was Spain. Throughout the reign of James I, Spain was the most powerful state in Europe; Spanish art and literature shone with their greatest brilliance; Spanish gravity and courtesy impressed all those who were not hostile in policy or in religion. King James was more open to Spanish advances than many of his counsellors or of his politically active subjects. There seems, however, to be only one thing in which he copied Spanish ways, and this was a recourse that arose naturally from his own character and circumstances, the practice of recognizing a royal favourite as the channel for patronage and for a large proportion of other public business. In Spain the favourite Olivares held great offices of state, and his position was but little different from that of the great ministers, Richelieu and Mazarin, later on, in France. The Jacobean system was one of several expedients by which King James tried to avoid the burden of government while yet maintaining unity in the direction of affairs. It failed because the two favourites were unequal to what was expected of them: Somerset's spell of power ended in personal disgrace, Buckingham's in public calamity. This was all that the Spanish example contributed to English constitutional development.

Soon after the civil war broke out it became evident that Spain was no longer the greatest power. France was taking her place, not only in power but in intellectual and social prestige, and England was brought into the French gravitational pull. In former centuries some of the major English institutions had been imported from France. Political relations with France fluctuated in interaction with British internal politics; and after 1660, under the two half-French sons of Charles I, there were not only determined supporters and determined opponents of a pro-French foreign policy; there was also a domestic policy of imitating France. The special institutions which France developed from the beginning of the century were those of absolute monarchy. The Stuarts would have liked to be absolute, but absolute monarchy cannot exist unless it has some institutions to connect the monarch with his submissive subjects. In France the power of the state was imposed by a bureaucratic administration. There were times in the reign of Charles II when it looked as if England could be governed in the same spirit and with similar institutions. In some small details perhaps the weak and rudimentary English bureaucracy was touched by French examples.[13] There were some among the ablest and boldest of Charles's ministers who believed that they could dispense with parliament and chartered right and rule England efficiently by means of an administrative hierarchy. The attempt was made, but parliament, the Church of England, the municipal corporations, the self-governing universities, and the counties held their ground. The French example failed to modify anything in the addiction of the English governing class to decentralization and amateur control.

It might have been expected that English institutions would take some considerable impress from the Dutch, as English economic and cultural life did. For the first half of the period, to be sure, there was fierce antagonism between the two nations, but it often happens that rivalry is the stimulus which leads to imitation. Later the two countries were allied, and even when they were rivals they had much in common. In each of them medieval representative institutions had survived the sixteenth-century hardening of monarchy; in each an established church had to find a *modus vivendi* with Romanist and sectarian dissent. Even if there were no corroboration from other sources, it would be unreasonable to doubt the opinion of Thomas Hobbes that many men, particularly in the city of London and other great towns of trade, admiring the prosperity of the Netherlands after they revolted from their sovereign the King of Spain, were 'inclined to think' that the like change of government would produce the like prosperity in England.[14] When England became a Puritan republic the Dutch were the first to give it diplomatic recognition. Its government surprised and embarrassed the Dutch by proposing a union of the two. The Dutch had long since put the Utopian fervours of revolution behind them, and instead of union they chose war; but the success of the Dutch revolt and the stability of the Dutch republic certainly encouraged and upheld the English republicans. The Levellers remembered them,[15] and the Dutch experience of toleration was held up as an example by men who knew it at first hand.[16] When the English experiment was ending in failure and recrimination John Milton wrote that its makers had 'left no memorial behind them but in the common laughter of Europe'. 'Which,' he went on, 'must needs the more redound to our shame, if we but look upon our neighbours of the United Provinces, to us inferior in all outward advantages, who notwithstanding in the midst of greater difficulties, courageously, wisely, constantly went through with this same work and are settled in all the happy enjoyments of a potent and flourishing republic to this day.'[17]

The Dutch constitution had one characteristic which may well seem to us to have been suitable for imitation here. It was a federal constitution, and it seems in retrospect that federation might have been the best framework for English relations with Scotland, Ireland

and even Wales. But it seldom occurred to Englishmen that this was a possibility. Their historical tradition was that of successive unions under the monarchy. They had no experience of federation. Dutch federalism had grown out of the immediate local circumstances of the Dutch war of independence. One famous political writer considered and rejected the federal plan. James Harrington wrote that Switzerland and Holland, commonwealths propagated and enlarged by equal leagues, were 'dangerous to themselves, precarious governments, such as do not command, but beg their bread from province to province, in coats that being patched up of all colours are in effect of none'.[18] That is nearly the same criticism as that of Alexander Hamilton and James Madison in the last decade of the Dutch confederation.[19] There were some who took a more favourable view, for instance William Penn, who knew Holland well, and was half-Dutch by birth.[20] In 1707, during the discussions preceding the union with Scotland, the Scots commissioners did discuss among themselves federation on the Dutch model as an alternative to 'entire union', one which would have been more agreeable to Scottish opinion, but they knew there was no possibility that the English would accept it.[21]

Imitation of the Dutch constitution as a whole was out of the question; but that did not exclude the imitation of details. On the borderline between government and economic life it can be traced. From the moment when the favourite Buckingham formed his warlike plans at the end of James I's reign, the advisers of the Crown began to think of new taxes copied from the Dutch and especially of an excise as a means of remedying the miserable state of the finances.[22] During the civil war both sides experimented with it. Finally, after the Restoration, the 'Dutch excise' became a permanent and major feature of English taxation. It was not the only Dutch tax to be transplanted. Stamp duties on legal documents probably also came from there. When, however, we move away from matters of money there seems to be only one principle of government which anyone even thought of taking over from Dutch practice. Constitution-makers in the time of the Commonwealth and Protectorate considered various schemes for making popular control over government more continuous than that of intermittent parliaments. Milton thought that the principle of perpetuity might save the English republic. He cited several examples of perpetual systems. The Jews, the Athenians, the Spartans, the Romans and the Venetians had all had governments which never interrupted their sittings, and among his examples the nearest home was that of the Dutch.[23] But nothing came of this. It was as alien to the English tradition as federalism. Oliver Cromwell as Protector had reverted to the Elizabethan arrangement of short parliamentary sessions. One of the great difficulties of parliamentary management in the Restoration period, partly solved by Danby, was the propensity of many members to disperse to their homes in the country before the business of the session was over.[24] Annual sessions became necessary when the great wars began in the reign of William III, but they were winter sessions. England never had a legislature, or even a government, like the Dutch states general which met all the year round and on seven days a week. Perpetuity was congenial only to states in which the towns predominated. Neither federation nor perpetuity suited the English, and it would be difficult to find any other Dutch political practice that was proposed as a model here.

By examining the impact of the three great states which might have been taken as models for imitation, we have seen that while English civilization was transformed by influences from abroad, its government and the institutions underwent no such process. There may indeed have been surreptitious influences which cannot be detected now, currents of ideas and patterns of conduct modifying political behaviour, but in their visible and recorded public life the English went their own way. Instead of being assimilated to any external principles, their system of law and order, of public finance and of administration in general, steadily diverged and became more unlike any other. Shall we be justified in saying that this was the crowning example of insularity? Not without attending to some other considerations, for it may well have struck you already that something not very dissimilar might be said of the development of the other European nations in the period. Scotland indeed was less Scottish at the end than at the beginning. But France was more

French; Holland was more Dutch; Brandenburg-Prussia was more Prussian and Eastern Europe was more unlike the West. The tragic reverse side of European achievement in the seventeenth century was that every addition to the strength and efficiency of a state was accomplished in forms that made mutual understanding and co-operation more arduous and more precarious. The conservatism and the growing idiosyncrasy of England were the local expression of a European destiny.

The local expression was, however, unique. It was determined in important respects by the insular position of the state. Great Britain alone among the great powers was safe enough to live for long stretches of years without keeping a standing army on foot in time of peace. From that it followed that Great Britain was the only region in Europe where revolution could be indulged in without opening the frontiers to invasion. Geography enabled common sense to guarantee prosperity, and strategic security sheltered the survival of innumerable anomalies and curiosities. In my two following lectures I shall comment on the social and political ethos of England itself.

NOTES

1 Sir Halford Mackinder, *Britain and the British Seas*, 2nd ed. (1930), pp. 357–8. The first edition was published in 1902.

2 D. L. W. Tough, *The Last Years of a Frontier* (1928).

3 Edmund Waller, *Panegyrick to my Lord Protector* (1655). In Waller's earlier poem to Charles I in his navy the emphasis is on insular safety:

> ''Tis not so hard for greedy foes to spoil
> Another nation as to touch our soil.'

4 Speech of 25 January 1657/8 in *Writings and Speeches of Oliver Cromwell*, ed. W. C. Abbott, iv (1947), 715.

5 George Savile, Marquis of Halifax, *A Rough Draft of a New Model at Sea*, published anonymously in 1694, p. 4.

6 See J. W. Stoye, *English Travellers Abroad, 1604–67* (1952).

7 A. M. Hind, *Rembrandt* (1932), pp. 15–17.

8 J. W. Muller, *De uitbreiding van het nederlandsch taalgebiet vooral in de 17ᵉ eeuw* (1939), esp. p. 93.

9 W. C. Braithwaite, *The Second Period of Quakerism* (1919), p. 452.

10 Lady Alice Archer-Houblon, *The Houblon Family* (1908), i. 207–8.

11 For this subject Kathleen Lambley, *The Teaching and Cultivation of the French Language in England during Tudor and Stuart Times* (1920), a work which also has some Dutch references, should be supplemented from M. H. Curtis, *Oxford and Cambridge in Transition* (1959), especially pp. 137–9.

12 The ingenious and learned work of the late Dr. A. A. van Schelven, *De Calvinisme in zijn bloetijd*, 2 vols. (1943–51), compares the Calvinist style of living in different countries. It was unfortunately not completed, but covers Geneva, France, Scotland, England, and North America.

13 The title of 'inspector' seems to have come into English official use from France in 1671 and to have become common between 1686 and 1702: E. Hughes in *History*, xxiv (1939), 270, but it was anticipated by no less a champion of freedom than John Milton: *Ready and Easy Way to establish a Free Commonwealth* (1659/60), Columbia Edition, vi (1932), 126. It was not with regard to its administration but with regard to its contents that he was 'to have an inspection into' the State Paper Office: J. Masson, *Life of Milton*, iv (1877), 145, 152, 157.

14 *Leviathan* (1651), p. 170; *Behemoth*, finished about 1668, published 1679, p. 168 in vol. vi of Sir William Molesworth's edition of Hobbes's *English Works* (1840).

15 See the reference by Richard Overton in 1647 in A. S. P. Woodhouse, *Puritanism and Liberty* (1938), p. 325.

16 For instance Hugh Peters, speaking immediately before Overton in the Whitehall debates of 1648, *ibid.*, p. 138.

17 *Ready and Easy Way*, p. 118.

18 *The Commonwealth of Oceana* (1656), p. 260.

19 *The Federalist*, Letter No. XX, 11 December 1787. Here the 'awful spectacle' of the Dutch crisis of that year is used to reinforce the lesson that the central legislative and executive authorities in a federation ought to govern the individual citizens directly. The summary description of the Dutch system is almost completely accurate.

20 *Essay towards the Present and Future Peace of Europe* (1693/4), in *Works* (1726), ii. 838 ff.

21 Sir John Clerk of Penicuik, *Memoirs*, ed. J. M. Gray (1895), p. 60.

22 S. R. Gardiner, *History of England* (ed. of 1908), v. 195–6 for 1624, vi. 222–3 for 1627. Bacon said a good word for the Dutch excise in *De Augmentis Scientiarum* (1623), bk. viii, c. 3

23 *Ready and Easy Way*, p. 129.

24 See the letter of Brian Duppa, 27 August 1660, in *The Correspondence of Bishop Brian Duppa and Sir Justinian Isham*, ed. by Sir Gyles Isham (*s.a.*, 1954), p. 185; A. Browning, *Thomas Osborne, Earl of Derby*, i (1951), 167; Tallard to Louis XIV, 12 June 1697, in A. Legrelle, *La diplomatie française et la succession d'Espagne*, ii (1889), 261.

II

Social Structure

WHEN A MODERN WRITER sets out to give a general account of any country, he usually begins with the figures of its area and population. The first generation of English statisticians, a small and remarkable group of pioneers who first attracted notice soon after the Restoration of Charles II, already practised this approach. A generation or so after these beginnings Gregory King made the first scientific estimate of the population of England and Wales, for which he arrived at the total of 5,500,520,[1] and Edmond Halley corrected the current estimates of the area by the sensible method of cutting out a large map and weighing it.

The early statisticians needed these outlines in order to work inwards to detailed problems of demography such as the expectation of life. They made good use of the materials they could come by. They used returns of the number of houses made in the course of collecting certain taxes, and also some not very satisfactory data about the numbers of deaths in London. Without a full census, which was never attempted until long after that time, they could not get much further, but Gregory King made some careful sample enumerations in selected places. From these he made calculations about the size of families in the different income groups and about the total numbers in these groups in the whole country. He worked for the Treasury, and one of his purposes was to forecast the yield of direct taxes. Except for this, the government had scarcely any motive for informing itself about these matters: it took no responsibility for sanitation, and there was not, as in Sweden and Prussia, any military conscription for which a knowledge of the numbers of age-groups was required. In Gregory King's time improvements were made in the registration of births and marriages, and registration was extended to cover not only baptisms in the Church of England but all live births. To that extent the materials were improved, but the purpose was still fiscal and by our standards the whole procedure was still primitively inexact.

When population studies entered on a new era after the first British census and the *Essay* of Malthus (1798), demographers wanted to know more about the earlier developments. For the earlier part of the seventeenth century information was scanty, but there was an immense, unco-ordinated mass of facts in the parish registers of baptisms and births, marriages and burials. These records were incomplete and in many ways unreliable, but successive registrars-general and other experts did their best to extract all that they could be made to yield. A third period of great activity in population-studies began in our own time, in the nineteen-thirties, and the old calculations have been revised in the light of new and better statistical technique. Gregory King's method has been closely examined, and such of his raw materials as survive are being studied. We now know more about the course of population movements in the Stuart period than anyone knew at that time.

We may in time come to know more still. We could probably arrive at a clearer picture if we could plan and execute, with the aid of electronic computers, a complete and thorough survey of the millions of entries in the parish registers. Whether we shall ever be able to afford such a major undertaking of research I do not like to foretell. At present our advance from Gregory King's position is disappointingly slight. We are not in a position to put forward any other estimate of the total population as certainly more credible than his. He does not command complete acceptance. His final figure would have looked better as an approximation if he had given round numbers and omitted the figures 520 at the end of it. He undermines our confidence by giving accompanying estimates of the numbers of animals. These indeed are in round figures, but it is hard to imagine how he arrived, for instance, at a million for the rabbits and 24,000 for hares and leverets. The best opinion now is that his figure for the human population represents the upper limit of probability, and that a deduction of 250,000–300,000 would probably be justified.[2] For the earlier history we may conclude provisionally that there was a slow but continuous increase of population from about the year 1500, and that there was an epoch of high birth-rates in England and Wales centring about 1600.[3]

If we had more definite knowledge of these matters, we should be able to understand some of the social history of the Stuart period more clearly, above all the emigration to America. It appears that by 1660 somewhere about 100,000 Englishmen had sailed away to the mainland colonies and the West Indies.[4] That movement coincided roughly in time with some emigration to Ireland and some internal colonization on drained marshes and improved waste lands. In trying to discover its nature we cannot begin as we should like to begin, from the facts of population year by year; we cannot correlate the facts of the exodus with evidence of pressure of population on the means of subsistence. We know that advocates of overseas settlement had argued from Elizabethan times that there was an excess of population; but we also know that this view was exceptional, and in all probability, so far as it argued that there was a general excess over the whole country, it was erroneous. From about the middle of the seventeenth century on a small scale there were various kinds of compulsory emigration. But for the crucial period we have to work outwards from the local units, not inwards from the circumference. In any case, however complete our knowledge may become, we shall always have to break down the national figures of emigrants into local, occupational, and religious groups, and we shall have to use direct knowledge of the individual emigrants to discover their ages and their family circumstances, to say nothing of their motives or their hopes. We do know a great deal about some of these matters already, but this concrete knowledge gains in stability wherever it can be related to statistical knowledge.

Historians down to the present have had no theory of population except the optimum theory, and that can no longer be regarded as adequate for their purposes.[4] There is one school of demographers, most prominent in France, who insist that even in this sphere abstract statistical study is not enough. A modern writer who demonstrated that there was an epoch of high birth-rates in England and Wales about the year 1600 also advanced the opinion, without giving any supporting argument, that this was an expression of race physiology. We may form hypotheses about fecundity from racial, or rather national, physiology statistically considered, but it would be a vast and uncertain undertaking to check them for the seventeenth century by information about the physiology of individuals or of families. On the other hand we have quantities of scattered information about some other characteristics of men and women in Stuart England which are relevant to the reproduction of the human race. Here and there, by one chance or another, we have data about contraception. There are books and sermons in which it is reprehended, and other writings in which it is condoned. We have masses of literary evidence about social attitudes to large and small families, to early and late marriages, to children and to childhood. Historians are beginning, but only beginning, to collect and survey this material. It may not be long before they add a new chapter to the history of Stuart England, the story of the partly conscious and partly unconscious control of population movement by custom and choice.

That significant chapter of human relationships may perhaps be pieced together from myriads of fragments. Not all of these fragments are isolated facts; sometimes they were linked together by thought. There were many people who thought in a primitive way about social structure, though only a few of the more systematic thinkers had anything resembling the notion that society is an interdependent whole built up of human associations of many kinds. In 1693 an economic pamphleteer threw out the remark that according to the 'reasonable opinion of the most intelligent men' the population of England, Scotland, Ireland and the American Plantations was ten millions.[5] That was not at all a bad shot, but the number of intelligent men who paid much attention to such matters was still very small. Most of the attempts which were made to explain how society was constituted showed no interest in numbers or quantities.

Many volumes and innumerable pamphlets were written which directly or indirectly described the structure of English society and explained how it had come into being. They contributed very little towards answering the questions which modern sociologists ask. They paid little attention to the economic groundwork of the subject. They started from those articulations of society which were most easily seen. On these they brought both learning and critical insight to bear. Everyone knew that there were wide differences of wealth and poverty, and equally wide differences of power and subjection. The wealthiest were not always the most powerful; the two sets of gradations did not exactly coincide, but there was some relation between them. Everyone also knew that society was in some way founded on the family; property was hereditary; kinship was one of the keys to power in every walk of life from the royal household down to the craft guild. From Aristotle downwards there had been political theorists who traced the origin of organized society to a union of families into tribes and of tribes into states. Churchmen had systematized the rules of marriage and consanguinity. Jurists had worked out doctrines about paternal power and the rights of succession to property. So at every level from naïve observation to scholarly theory there were social ideas which were centred on the family.

A second obvious fact about English society was that it had been formed by the union of peoples speaking different languages. The Stuart period bred excellent historians who taught the English many things about their past. The great classics of Greek and Roman history, and also the historical books of the Old Testament, narrated early history in terms of tribes and races, and English historians told their own island story, as many historians still tell it, as a story of Ancient Britons, of Anglo-Saxons and of Normans. The Celtic languages of Wales, the Isle of Man and

Cornwall, brought the story down to their own time. So did Law French, the debased Anglo-Norman language in which the principles of the Common Law were still concealed from the uninitiated populace. It was not altogether unscientific to ascribe many institutions, and especially those which upheld social inequality, to the yoke imposed by the Norman Conquest. There was indeed a brisk and endless controversy about the yoke. Some thought it beneficent, some thought it oppressive; it was as much myth as history, like the conflict of Celt and Teuton; but in one form or another it was the accepted historical explanation of the main lines of English society.[6]

There was another stream of ideas which united with these, the stream of heraldry and genealogy. Interwoven with the distinctions of wealth and power, and even more plainly visible, was the elaborately systematized distinction of ranks. From the king and the dukes as far down as the gentleman, every person had the right to acquire an emblazoned coat of arms. In the Middle Ages the distinctions of rank were closely related to rights, privileges, duties and burdens. Heralds and other officers of arms controlled the whole system by inspection and by adjudicating in disputes over armorial bearings and precedence. It is only recently, through the happy discovery of two large boxfuls of papers in a storeroom at the College of Arms, that we have come to understand what a solid constitutional fact was enunciated by Sir John Keeling, Chief Justice of the King's Bench, when he said as late as 1668 that the court of chivalry was 'part of the law of England'.[7] The heralds were active all over the country on their visitations, and they collected information about the people who claimed arms and titles of honour, and especially about their families. There were famous historians among these professional genealogists, for instance William Camden, in the first rank, and Sir William Dugdale, well below it. They left behind them certified pedigrees which showed where each individual stood in the line of descent by which the right to bear arms was transmitted. Unfortunately the heralds took fees for making these, and some heralds ministered unscrupulously to family pride and personal vanity. Their standards of evidence would not have satisfied the courts of law, which had to decide on the succession to property. They awarded far too often the supreme distinction of having come over with the Conqueror. Nevertheless their records have been the delight of local historians from that day to this, and it is largely owing to them that most of the county histories of England for 200 years were primarily histories of the county families. These were the chief landed families of a mainly agricultural society. Their genealogies supply a framework for the history of land-owning. One man's estate was enlarged by marriage with a landed heiress, another's divided to provide for his children, or impoverished by litigation over the succession: events like these left their marks in the family tree, and although there were many other relevant events which did not concern the heralds, such as sales and purchases, and the acquisition of wealth from other sources than the land, these agrarian facts taken together constituted a valuable body of historical information.

Information of this kind was, however, of more circumscribed value for the Stuart period than for the Middle Ages. As the wealth and population of the country grew, the proportion of people employed on the land declined and so did the proportion of the national wealth which the land represented. Commerce and industry grew. The distinctions of rank were less closely related to distinctions of wealth, power, function and obligation. The peers still constituted one house of parliament; they still had privileges and exemptions, and their families, though primogeniture prevented them from forming a noble caste, were still socially superior to everyone else. But outside the circle of the peerage there were many men of substance whose position was not formalized by anything which the heralds recorded. To take the best-known example, King Charles I tried to compel all those of his subjects who had the necessary qualifications to accept the honour of knighthood; but he did not succeed. In the Long Parliament of 1640, there was a direct attack on the legality of the court of chivalry, opened by Edward Hyde, afterwards Earl of Clarendon, and led by John Pym. It was one sign among others that the old system of degree no longer adequately expressed the realities of the social order.

Normanism and genealogy were both compatible with the long-standing belief that men's places in society were determined by inherited differences like those of the different breeds of dogs and horses. There were, however, other current beliefs which could not be reconciled with this. The great majority of people in the seventeenth century believed that the whole human race was descended from Adam and Eve. That popular belief had furnished an egalitarian argument for the Peasants' Revolt in the fourteenth century. One of the earlier writers whose books were classics for Stuart England, Edmund Spenser, who died in 1600, wrote that a man's manners would show of what degree and what race he was grown, but he also wrote that a new-born child might be engraved with any qualities of character and mind.

> And certes it hath oftentimes been seene
> That of the like whose image was unknowne,
> More brave and noble knights have raised beene . . .
> Than those which have been dandled in the lap.[8]

But it was so hard to accommodate this fact to his beliefs that he suggested these heroes might be changelings.

Neither Normanism nor genealogy could explain the already very complicated structure of English society. Neither of them took sufficient account of the movements of families upwards or downwards from one social grade to another, which anyone could watch in his own environment.

A clergyman, who also practised medicine and was interested in things in general, wrote in his commonplace book: 'England hath been so often shuffled from high to low, that scarce any artificer but may find his name, though not his pedigree, in the heralds' college books.'[9] There is a fallacy here, the fallacy of thinking that all men with the same surname are akin. Another superficially similar though essentially different argument also tending to minimize the significance of heredity as a cause of social stratification rests on a different fallacy. This professes to prove that everyone living in England at the present day must be lineally descended from everyone who was living there at the time of the Norman Conquest. The principle of this latter argument is to be found in no less august a work than Blackstone's *Commentaries*,[10] but I doubt whether it had been invented in Stuart times. It is still current.

It might have been expected that modern historians with their improved technique would put the data accumulated in the seventeenth century into shape and use them as the basis of a sociological interpretation. They have indeed provided us with a far more accurate view of the aspects of society which interested Stuart England. They have eliminated much that was slipshod, much that was even fraudulent in the old pedigrees. They have studied the effects of the development of law on the accumulation and maintenance of landed estates. They have not, at least on any extended scale, drawn inferences about the geographical movements of families, or about social mobility between occupations and levels of welfare. So far as I can hear they have not attempted what might be called scientific genealogy, or a study of the family as an institution.[11] Taken with other materials genealogy may tell us how often a line of a given number of generations, whether reckoned directly through males, or reckoned through females, is to be found seated on the same land. It may help us to discover the number of children born to marriages, and the proportion which survived to maturity. It may throw light on the obscure but not uninteresting question how the family was conceived in different portions of the population, what degree of cousinship was held to make a relative, and how large were the family groups to which people felt they belonged. More ambitiously it may possibly be used to check some of the downright statements of writers on eugenics and genetics about the biological inheritance of human characteristics. We have indeed no more than scraps of information about the physique of a few exceptional people who lived in the seventeenth century. Even of these something might be made. Some geneticists put forward opinions which do not depend on precise physical knowledge, for instance Sir Ronald Fisher's view that successful men in all classes produce fewer progeny than less successful men.[12] This can be tested historically.

Eugenist theories rest largely on principles of inheritance which scientists agree in accepting, but these cannot be seen in operation except in relatively simple, indeed odd and exceptional cases. Nevertheless, the scientists confidently tell us that there is scarcely any social custom or legislative act which does not produce some genetic effects. If this is so now, something like it must have been true to some degree then, and if we know nothing about that, then a chapter is missing from our history. It is a disappointment and a challenge to historians of the seventeenth century that the great Royal Commission on Population which reported in 1951 began its historical review at 1700, a mere eight or nine generations ago, a very short span in our biological history.

Our knowledge of seventeenth-century social structure is advancing, though it keeps to the beaten track. Economic historians are adding to our knowledge of the business world and its affairs. Local historians are setting out, family by family and estate by estate, the facts of agrarian history. County by county we are learning to understand social relationships. It will still be many years before we can expect a well-proportioned survey of the social structure of the country as a whole; but we need provisional conclusions as a framework for the detailed studies. In this framework the first main upright should be an estimate of the importance of London. England was mainly agricultural, with growing industries for domestic consumption and for export; but it was dominated, so far as the state of transport and communications then permitted, by London. Perhaps a tenth of the whole population lived there. In London and the adjoining suburbs and towns there were concentrated not only the greatest port of the kingdom, the metropolitan markets for some of the chief commercial commodities such as wool, corn, and tin, but finance and the government of church and state. Centralization as we know it was still impossible, and there were survivals of the times when the only way to control a large area was to move about in it; but even at the beginning of the period London was more than ten times bigger than the largest provincial town and powerful in a far greater proportion. We may say that everything centred there except higher education. Oxford and Cambridge were the only two places where independent thought and ways of life were so well-rooted that statesmen and leaders of opinion had to take them into account. It was symbolic of their status that they were the only two places outside London where printing presses were allowed; but in printing they had only a small share of the business, and even in some parts of education, especially in the law, London overshadowed them.

London itself grew and its predominance grew in every respect all through the Stuart period. It may be disputable to say that it had the strongest municipality in Europe; it would be an exaggeration to say that England was becoming simply the environment of its capital; but it is more nearly true of the seventeenth and eighteenth centuries than of any other that every generalization about the social structure of the country must be controlled by relating it to this primary fact.

The next set of facts which have to be co-ordinated with this are the facts relating to social groupings, and here, as with population, the most convenient starting-point is in the tables of Gregory King. Following a habit which was already a century old among his unmethodical predecessors, he classified the population, still having in mind his main purpose of forecasting how much could be extracted from it by taxation. He gives twenty-six headings, defined partly by wealth, but partly also by rank and by legal status. The first five headings go purely by rank, each rank having a standard income assigned to it, for instance £880 to the 800 baronets, but there were many squires who were richer than many of the baronets, and rank was no longer a criterion of wealth or power. As it happened King was himself Lancaster Herald, and it is possible that this professional interest led him to overrate the relevance of the scale of ranks to his fiscal and sociological studies. If so, that may partly excuse him; what is less excusable is the preservation of this scale by modern writers, even including Russians. It was an element in the structure of society, and it deserves to be studied for its own sake; but in comparison with wealth and ability it was a minor element even then, and too much attention to it tends to exaggerate the social influence of the state. But if the notions of heraldry interfere with our view of these relations, so does the fully-formed notion of class as applied to the period of high capitalism.

In the seventeenth-century social structure there was indeed an upper class, or rather there were upper classes, and they were strongly marked by exclusiveness in regard to marrying beneath them. One thing which distinguished them was that some of their members had public functions, but so had many of their inferiors, down to the substantial householders who were liable to serve as jurors and village constables. The dividing line between those who had social functions and those who had not came very low down in the scale. A considerable portion of those below whom it was drawn—tens of thousands of 40*s.* freeholders in the counties and thousands of burgesses in the towns —were legally but not economically or socially distinguished from greater numbers of similar men. They had parliamentary votes, and some of them exercised this franchise with some degree of responsibility. Thus the political power of the commons was partly derived from this large complex of classes. Together with those who were thus excluded by chance from political functions, we may say that the classes with social functions amounted to something like one-quarter of the whole. King did not divide the men of law or the officers of the two services or the practitioners of the liberal arts and sciences horizontally as he did the placemen, merchants and clergy, and that draws our attention to the fact that ways of life and community of interests in many cases followed the vertical, not the horizontal divisions. The governing classes were stratified by wealth and heraldry, but the social position of a man and his family and his attitude to public affairs, might depend less on whether he had an income of £1,000 a year than on whether he was a 'mere landowner', a judge, a merchant or a general.

Lower down in the scale the same held good. There

was a large body (reckoned by King at 12,000) of gentlemen, which seems to mean landed gentlemen. Below them one of King's distinctions is between freeholders of the lesser sort with £55 and farmers with £42. 10*s*.; another is between persons in liberal arts and sciences with £60, shopkeepers and tradesmen with £45; but it is incredible that, even if these averages were fully justified, there were not many shopkeepers who were better off than many schoolmasters. Towards the bottom of the scale it was still the case that the vertical divisions were as important as the horizontal. The industrious apprentice married his master's daughter; the journeyman and the master in one craft felt a stronger antagonism to a rival craft than to a propertyless proletariat or to capitalistic oppressors. There was no working class in the modern sense; still less was there an organized working-class movement. The nation was graded into strata, but it was also partitioned by functions. The simplest parallel is perhaps that of an army, in which there are divisions of rank but also divisions into regiments. Each set of divisions coincides with a fabric of habits, sentiments and interests.

All these distinctions were gradual and they were all fluid. Nothing could counteract the tendency of private property and freedom of contract to make some men grow richer and others poorer. The scope of this tendency was restricted by the laws of inheritance, especially regarding land, but it remained very wide. The growth of population and wealth brought with them, as growth always does, specialization of functions. In addition to these causes, another operated which increased the number and diversity of the jobs which had to be done, namely the growth, step by step, of the armed forces and of the administrative and economic organization behind them. It appears that the final result was to weaken the vertical and emphasize the horizontal divisions, a process which went much further in the two following centuries. One contrast which was weakened was that between the landed and the moneyed interest. At the beginning of the period the two were distinct, indeed they had little social contact except in the nature of transactions. Right down to the end of the period some politicians and some pamphleteers tried to appeal to one against the other; but it was absolutely proved by writers like Defoe that by that time they were inextricably intermingled. Their interests had become fused in the common interests of the governing class. Another instance is that of the Church of England. At the accession of James I, in spite of its acute disagreements and of the poverty of the lower clergy, the church was a powerful interest. By Queen Anne's time its Convocation had ceased to do any business; the church interest was weakened by the stability of nonconformity outside it. 'The church in danger' was still a political cry at election times. But the clergy married, and grade for grade they married as suited their places in the social hierarchy. The church was ceasing to be a separate interest and becoming a graduated annex of the gentry and the aristocracy.

This hardening of the horizontal divisions was proceeding, and one factor was the rise of the middling classes. Their members became more numerous; the rewards of success became greater for them; their functions became more specialized. New types of middle-class men emerged, such as paid scientists, and journalists. In the City the occupations of dealers in money were divided and subdivided. There were accountants, most of whom taught accountancy as well as keeping books for clients. Perhaps fewer of them now taught writing and arithmetic as well. In the lower branch of the legal profession attorneys were more clearly distinguished from solicitors, and the species of solicitors were separated. Both branches of the medical profession advanced in numbers and prestige: there were great improvements in the treatment of disease, and the rewards of successful practice became greater. The army was virtually a new profession, and it was specially attractive to the younger sons of gentlemen. It became much less common for them to be apprenticed to business men in London and the provincial towns. Thus, with the church, the bar and the army open to them, and, less widely or easily, the navy, they came to be further apart from the business world. The vertical division between business and the professions became clearer, but at the same time the professions became more hierarchical and these hierarchies fitted into the general social scale so as again to emphasize the horizontal stratification.

During the Stuart period there was no great advance

in professional organization, the association of practitioners to promote their interests in relation to clients. On the other hand the professions owed nothing of their improved position to encouragement given by the state. They did not, on the whole, advance their interests as they had done in earlier times, and were to do in later, by asking for chartered privileges. They flourished in a freedom which had perhaps no parallel on the continent except in the Netherlands. An American historian has shown convincingly and in detail that there had been a revolution in the function of the two universities. From about the time of Queen Elizabeth I they had increasingly made it their business not only to train the clergy, but to give a wide and flexible education to the laity, and especially to country gentlemen and those who followed the professions.[13] England now had middle classes with social power and influence, though not yet with a sense of common interest.

The counterpart of this change, the depression of the aristocracy, was not a simple movement, and indeed the Georgian aristocracy, having laid new foundations for its power became dominant in its turn; but for contemporaries the most astonishing event of the Stuart period was the collapse of the established order in the revolution which began in 1640. During the last sixteen years or so there has been a vigorous controversy in which historians have thrown out new and conflicting theories about how the civil wars came about and why the king was beaten.[14] They have added much to our knowledge of social structure, though we cannot yet be sure how much. They have done it indirectly because their interest is in social structure not in itself but as a determinant of political action. They apply to the seventeenth century the methods by which Professor Tout analysed medieval administration, those by which economic historians traced the ups and downs of large and small landowners, those by which Sir Lewis Namier has elucidated the workings of eighteenth-century representative institutions and Sir John Neale has depicted the Elizabethan political scene. For the present, however, their work has for the most part been concentrated on the years from the accession of James I to the restoration of Charles II. They deal with political men, and their tendency is to investigate the economic position of a class, then to deduce what its interests were, and, lastly taking an individual, to place him in his class and by discovering how he made his way in public life, how he spoke and voted, to decide whether he followed these interests. For some of these writers the political man is a sub-species of the economic man, distinguished only by a less simple appetite.

The unending struggle for office and power leaves behind it materials which reveal actions and motives, stresses and antagonisms, concealed in the overt proceedings of public life. The network of mutual obligations among politicians, the bargains which turned on ambition or cupidity, the traffic in honours and offices and emoluments, the bribes, the blackmail, the deceptive promises and the voluntary or reluctant 'clientage' seem to form an underlying foundation more real than the edifice which contemporaries saw above the surface. But there are other elements of general history with which this view must be synthesized. No one indeed pretends that the structure of politics can furnish the whole explanation of political history. No one ignores the play of personalities, and the effects of mutual regard between two men, or mutual exasperation. No one denies the importance of ideas or principles, such as Puritanism in its many varieties, though some try to explain away these too as the outcome of interests. It is harder to fall into this error in the seventeenth century than in some others, but even on the political plane the analysis of interests leaves a great unresolved residuum.

From the social point of view the means by which men attain office and power are the means by which certain functions are allotted to individuals. In our large and complex societies it is a matter of the utmost importance that they shall be allotted to men who are capable of performing them well. In the simple world of the seventeenth century it did not matter so much. Functions were far less specialized than they are now. There was little need for special capacity or special training. With few exceptions every position in public and private business could be adequately filled by an average man taken at random from the governing class. Appointments could safely be made with far less study and precaution than we normally devote to them now, and perhaps society could afford a more generous portion of intrigue and corruption. But it is also true that English society was watchful in these matters, for the plain reason that competition for office and power is subsidiary to the exercise of office and power, and society had reached a stage in which it had the means and the will to insist on efficiency in high places. The rise and fall of each political leader deserves our attention because of the decisions he took once he had risen and until he fell. In the same way the soldiers were nearly all ambitious men, but what makes them interesting is not their promotions and commands but the battles they won or lost. The whole governing class and many who were outside it acquired some notion of the purport of major events, and so they had standards by which to judge the leaders. Victory in the struggle for power was insecure because, whatever the constitutional system of the time might be, society judged whether its work was well done. The test of success for the king's servants was not only whether they gained fame and fortune but how they served the king. One of the reasons why politics in Stuart England were violent and revolutionary was that the nation—if I may for once use a term which some people regard as meaningless—the nation was sensitive to mismanagement in high places.

A larger proportion of the English, and perhaps the Scottish, people than of any other was politically conscious. This would have been true even if only the governing class had been politically conscious, but there were also the religious dissidents who found themselves in collision with the authorities of the state. The circle widened. It spread to the rank and file of the parliamentary army, who had left their homes freely or under compulsion to live in billets and bivouacs with men who were fighting in a political and religious civil war. Political consciousness implied conceptions of the nature and purposes of the political community, and it implied standards for judging political conduct. It implied from the beginning that the king's servants, the servants of the symbolic head of the state, were public men, with responsibilities of which the public might judge. When the king himself came, like Strafford, to be tried for his life the standards were those which distinguished the just ruler from the tyrant, and so the whole body of political theory came into debate. For lesser people and on more ordinary occasions the standards were the everyday standards by which each man was judged in his calling. It was not a peculiarity of the Puritans to regard well-doing in his calling as one of the tests of a man's worth; it was and is a universally valid test, and a politically conscious nation applied it to its public men. In such a world there was a correlative desire on the side of those who held office and power and promoted others to it, the desire to do their work well. They might aim at anything from humdrum discipline and efficiency to high political achievement; their good intentions might be diluted or frustrated by defects of character or intelligence; but unless we recognize their sense of vocation we shall misinterpret their careers.

The determination to serve well has had many names and many varieties, two of which were prevalent in those times. The first was loyalty. In the earlier Stuart reigns an opposition developed between those who were ruled by a simple personal loyalty to the king as the embodiment of the state, and those who were loyal to something impersonal or at any rate not symbolized by any one person, a cause, religious or constitutional or both. Since a cause was not purely personal each of them had to follow his own interpretation of it, and there were many conflicting interpretations. Each could be fused with conscious or unconscious motives of self-seeking; but that was also true of the simple loyalty to the king. We know from tragic examples like that of Sir Edmund Verney that the conflict of loyalties could be as intense within the mind of one man as it was on the field of Edgehill where he died.[15] We are apt to think of loyalty as passionate and picturesque like our mental picture of the cavalier. The word does indeed come down from the age of chivalry, and it is not found in the Authorized Version of the Bible; but the thing itself was not romantic; it was as stern as any other aspect of duty, and it was not the private possession of either party.

In the course of the century a new phrase came into common use, which proved to be well suited to the changing temper of the times and to the constitutional balance in which the monarchy came to be organically united with other elements of society. This was the phrase 'public spirit'. So far as I know no one gave an adequate definition of it or expatiated on it at length. A reader who hopes to find anything of that kind in the *Essay upon Public Spirit* published by John Dennis in 1711 will be disappointed. Dennis treated it as equivalent to love of country, and his essay is a poor thing, a literary exercise appealing to the vulgar prejudice against foreigners. It deserves the sneer implied by Swift three years later when he entitled a pamphlet *The Public Spirit of the Whigs*. But public spirit was a fact more significant than anything that was written about it. It did induce men to sacrifice their own ease and advantage to the public. Like loyalty it was a component in some incongruous mixtures of motives, but even then it set up service to the public, the community, as the criterion of benefactions and of political activities. A forgotten scholar wrote in the time of the Protectorate: '*Public persons* with *private Aimes* are *Monsters* in *Church* or *State*. *Private Persons* with *publike Spirits* are of a *goodnesse Angelicall* . . . the *Spirit of Charity*; the *old Word* for *publike Spiritednesse* on which that Chapter I Cor. 13 is a *Commentary*.'[16] Even when they were written these words had an old-fashioned ring, but they state a permanent truth.

NOTES

1 For early editions of the tables see George Chalmers's edition of King's *Observations* (1804) and C. Davenant, *Works*, ed. Sir C. Whitworth (1771), ii. 184.

2 See P. E. Jones and A. V. Judges, 'London Population in the Late Seventeenth Century' in *Economic History Review*, vi (1935), 45 ff., and D. V. Glass in *Eugenics Review*, vi (1946), 170 ff., and *Population Studies*, iii (1950), 338 ff., and the literature referred to in these articles.

3 J. Brownlee, 'History of the Birth and Death Rates in England and Wales taken as a whole from 1756 to the Present Time', in *Public Health*, xix (1916), 211, 228, 237, and Sir Edward Gonner in *Statistical Journal*, lxxxvi (1922), 26.

4 The theory is usually formulated in some such words as those of Sir Alexander Carr-Saunders, *Population* (1922), p. 270: 'Under any given conditions there is a certain density of population which is the most desirable.' A more precise formula, connecting the total number of people with the principle of maximum return for labour, is given by E. Cannan, *Wealth* (2nd ed., 1924), but is omitted from the third edition (1928). I have reason to think that Professor Cannan made this omission in consequence of criticisms on the following lines: (1) the optimum human population for a given area can seldom or never be a simple figure, but is the aggregate of independently varying local, functional or other optima, (2) it is never possible in practice to vary the numbers or density of population without also changing other social conditions, (3) the optimum principle may easily be misinterpreted as implying that the individuals of which a population is composed are not ends but means to social ends.

5 *An Impartial Enquiry into the Advantages and Losses that England hath received since the beginning of this present War with France* (1693), p. 2.

6 For two short accounts of Normanism from different points of view see D. Douglas, *The Norman Conquest and British Historians* (1946), and J. E. C. Hill, *Puritanism and Revolution* (1958), pp. 50 ff.

7 All previous works on this subject must now be corrected from G. D. Squibb, *The High Court of Chivalry* (1959). See also P. H. Hardacre, 'The Earl Marshal, the Heralds and the House of Commons, 1604–41', in *International Review of Social Studies*, ii (1957), 106 ff.

8 *Faerie Queene*, Bk. VI, cantos iii, iv.

9 *Diary of the Rev. John Ward, 1648–79*, ed. C. Severn (1839), p. 288. If this was copied from some book it may possibly have been from Thomas Fuller, from whom Ward copied other entries.

10 First ed. 1765, ii. 203–4. The fallacy is exposed by W. Farr, Letter to the Registrar General in *Supplement to the 35th Annual Report of the Registrar General* (1875). I have to thank Professor D. J. Finney for this reference. Blackstone's first published work was a tract on *Collateral Consanguinity* (1750), which uses the reverse and correct argument to show that in the course of generations an absurdly large number of people would be able to claim the privileges of Founder's Kin at All Souls. The reign of George III was signalized by three other notorious public appearances of the doctrine of series in geometrical progression, Thelusson's Act (1800), Richard Price's *Appeal to the Public on the subject of the National Debt* (1771), and Malthus's *Essay on Population* (1798).

11 An example on a small scale is T. H. Hollingsworth, 'A Demographic Study of British Ducal Families' in *Population Studies*, xi (1957) 4 ff.

12 *The Social Selection of Human Fecundity* (1932), p. 28.

13 M. H. Curtis, *Oxford and Cambridge in Transition, 1558–1642* (1959).

14 For two summaries of the controversy, with references to the different articles, see J. E. C. Hill, *Puritanism and Liberty* (1958), pp. 3 ff.; J. H. Hexter in *Encounter*, x (1958), pp. 22 ff. G. E. Aylmer in *History*, xliv (1959), pp. 228 ff., and in his forthcoming book, *The King's Servants: the Civil Service of Charles I*, injects new facts into the controversy.

15 Edward Hyde, Earl of Clarendon, *Life* (1759), ii. 66 ff.

16 R. Whitlock, *Ζωοτομία* (1654), p. 382. G. Williamson in *Philological Quarterly*, xv (1936), gives the few available facts about Whitlock and his book.

III

Freedom

THESE LECTURES commemorate the life and work of Dr. Howard Primrose Whidden, and for that reason I shall devote the last of them to some considerations on freedom in seventeenth-century England. Dr. Whidden was a Baptist minister; two of the greatest and also of the most typical names in Baptist history are those of John Bunyan, who suffered bravely under religious persecution, and Roger Williams, the author of one of the classical statements of the case against persecution, whose privilege it was to put his belief into practice in North America. Their successors in England form one of those societies which we call 'the free churches' because they are immune from such control as the state exercises over the Church of England; and they have been champions of freedom in wider senses than this. Their newspaper in England, *The Baptist Times and Freeman*, carries as its motto a line of Cowper: 'He is the freeman whom the truth makes free.'

That Baptists and others among the seventeenth-century Puritans stood up for freedom in both these senses and in yet others resulted not from any historical accident but from the nature of their beliefs. Sometimes, however, it is difficult to see how they understood the connexion of these beliefs with freedom, and this difficulty becomes much greater if we move into the wider circles of seventeenth-century utterances about freedom. Whenever John Selden, the great scholar and lawyer, the independent-minded assertor of constitutional liberties, acquired a book he always wrote his motto in Greek on the fly-leaf. His books are in the Bodleian Library in Oxford now, and sometimes, as I have opened one of them to read, I have wondered exactly what was in his mind when he chose that motto: 'Freedom above everything.' It has a defiant ring, and yet few of his contemporaries would have deliberately rejected it. One example will show how easily we may be misled if we assume that the same key-words about freedom always mean similar things. Modern scholars search for early examples of the idea of natural liberty, a central idea in free-trade economics. In his answer to the Grand Remonstrance of 1641 King Charles I called the choice of his councillors and ministers of state 'the natural liberty all freemen have, and the undoubted right of the Crown'.[1] Perhaps this claim of freedom for the Crown was put in this form in order to score a debating point by turning their own weapon against Charles's opponents; but in the straightforward argument of his last speech on the scaffold he still represented himself as a defender of freedom. 'For the people, truly I desire their liberty and their freedom as much as anybody whatsoever; but I must tell you, their liberty and freedom consist in having good government, those laws by which their lives and goods may be most their own. It is not their having a share in the government; that is nothing appertaining to them. A subject and a sovereign are clear different things.'[2] Men in authority are always tempted to set bounds to liberty. Oliver Cromwell believed that after saving grace freedom was the 'next best God hath given men in this world', but in 1647 he went as far as Charles I when he said of the people: 'That's the question: what is for their good, not what pleases them.'[3]

We have to concede that men who fought on opposite sides believed with equal honesty that they were fighting for freedom. This happened the more easily because, with the single exception of national freedom from foreign rule, every species of civil and religious liberty became an issue in politics or even in war. By the end of the period it was a common belief, a common boast, that the English were more free than other nations. Until someone proves the contrary I am willing to believe it, but I wish to consider wherein this English freedom consisted.

It may well be that the English had profited more than others from a certain kind of political education. We saw that a larger proportion of the nation were politically conscious in England than elsewhere. This political consciousness was not of recent origin, nor were its earliest manifestations peculiar to England. The medieval institutions in the towns, the guilds and municipal corporations, carried on their business in meetings. In the countryside also there were meetings of the villages which decided on the affairs of the fields and animals, and no doubt decided after discussion. There was discussion even in bodies which acted under a lord: in the manorial court, for instance, there was a jury and it must have discussed its findings. Discussion is a means of arriving at the best decision, but it is much more than that. It implies some sort of equality between those who take part in it. To give a man a fair hearing is to pay him respect. When he speaks he will be judged by something more besides his status and his wealth or influence: he will be judged by what he says, and his native worth will make its impression. There can be no real discussion without this elementary kind of equality and this germ of fraternity. From that atmosphere two precious things may easily arise, tolerance and opportunity for talent. We know that it had been so in England for ages. I shall not venture to say how long, but I note that a learned authority on Domesday Book has recently ended a paragraph about the hundred and shire courts with these words: 'even in the assemblies of the eleventh century, men who were proud, selfish and violent might now and again, perhaps not infrequently, discover that their interests could be advanced more effectively by persuasion and compromise than by reliance upon force. Discussion is the great political educator.'[4]

In the sixteenth century, under the Tudors, so far as we can tell the habit of discussion in public affairs gained in strength and widened its scope. The Reformation led to much intellectual activity; literacy was increasing; many religious and charitable institutions, whether newly-founded or reorganized, were managed by boards consisting largely of laymen, and the proportion of the educated element among the laity increased. We cannot assign quantitative shares to these several causes; for instance, we cannot say whether discussion in religious congregations reinforced the habit of discussion as much as it did in Scotland; but there is little doubt about the fact of its growth, and this is the more important because it was only in this matter of discussion that Tudor England was a free country internally at all. The freedom which inspired the Elizabethans was their hard-won freedom from Spain and Rome. For this they paid the price of being subjected to prerogative courts which overruled the normal operation of law, to spying and arbitrary imprisonment, and to the repression of all dissent in religion. Even discussion was sternly limited by such laws as that against treason by words; but it was not discountenanced in itself. It went on, and from time to time in a parliament it was allowed to touch on some of the highest national concerns.

The Stuarts took over a difficult inheritance from the Tudors, with discontent not only among the Roman Catholics and the Puritans, but also among the peasantry. James I and Charles I did not initiate any essential changes in the machinery of the Tudor state. They added no new devices for coercion, but, although for a quarter of a century they were able to use the old devices much more moderately than Queen Elizabeth, they kept them all in action or in reserve, and they irritated legally-minded critics by announcing sharp-edged doctrines of their constitutional powers. King James I succeeded in remaining at peace with his neighbours. He continued, though not consistently or efficiently, the system of keeping down the influence of the nobility and employing men who had no inherited feudal power, and he was able to manage the magnates by distributing favours instead of by punishments and confiscations. But he did not solve his greater problems, especially, in his later years, his financial problems. He never gained the co-operation of parliament. Unlike his predecessor he did not keep the house of commons informed and controlled by competent privy councillors.[5] This omission was part of a wider negligence. His only constructive innovations were the system of favourites, and a few unpopular attempts at creating new officers to enforce economic regulations. He did not reform or build up the administrative system. At least in some of the counties there were educated country gentlemen with experience in public affairs who could have been used to greater advantage.[6] They found no road open to ambition except that of asserting themselves in parliament. The king could not do without the support of London, but his methods of obtaining it, for instance in the colonization of Ulster, promised little for the future. During his reign the demands for greater freedom developed somewhat, but they were still specific and sectional. The religious minorities hoped for mitigations of the laws against them; parliament insisted more obstinately on its privileges; but there was no comprehensive movement against the continuation of the Tudor system.

During the first few years of Charles I, the period of Buckingham's ascendancy, the Jacobean system was subjected to the strains of war and war-finance. All its weaknesses were exposed, and there was a preliminary instalment of parliamentary revolution. The Petition of Right made the first breaches in the institutional structure. Its plain intention was to tie the executive to a specific legal interpretation of its powers, and to weaken its power of military coercion. This portent was not understood. For the next eleven years the king tried to govern, and to pay the expenses of government, without a parliament. At the same time he tried to impose uniformity in the church. Whether, as many believed, he actually broke the letter of the law is a question which the legal historians have come to decide almost wholly in his favour. He made some not very important attempts at a policy of economic welfare. But he alienated many men, great and small, who were no more peccant than their neighbours. He alienated London. He did all this without the one instrument which might have given him success. Except for tax-collecting, coinage and the navy he had no administrative machine worth the name. His control over his own servants was imperfect. They in turn gave orders to authorities in the counties and boroughs whom they could not compel. His strongest minister, Strafford, had come over from parliamentary opposition with no training in the work of national government.

He and Laud drove blindly on until the Scots resisted. Then the Stuart system fell.

The revolution of 1640 was carried out by a parliament, and the freedom which it established, though it was soon engulfed in civil war, remained as part of the law of the land, standing fast at the Restoration of 1660 when the waves subsided. The prerogative courts were abolished, and this was the critical decision, afterwards supplemented and interpreted by others, which created the modern English constitutional monarchy, monarchy under the rule of law. On this foundation liberty of the person, of property and of religion could be built; without it they could all be revoked. But, although the foundation was laid, it took nearly half a century of strife to set up the building. The attacks on episcopacy gave King Charles a new following as defender of the Church of England. His opponents, with London and the navy on their side, were victorious; but they quarrelled among themselves and, so far as it was about principles that they quarrelled, it was about religious and constitutional freedom. Confusion reached such extremities that every grievance of the dispossessed, and every Utopian plan of the enthusiasts for freedom seemed to be within the sphere of practical politics. For one short period of suspended crisis it seemed as if a tolerant democratic republic would stand firm, masking military rule. Oliver Cromwell, as 'the constable set to keep the peace in the parish', brought back a provisional parliamentary monarchy, with a reformed franchise, a remarkable degree of *de facto* toleration, and a promise that the law-courts and the national morals should be reformed. Bitterly as the extremists of various colours resented what they thought his betrayal, by the standards of that violent age he used singularly little physical force against them. He personified both the old English political dispositions and the Puritan experiment; but no one else combined the two and when he died the experiment collapsed in anarchy.

General Monck gained the army and gained London. The monarchy was restored with all its traditional symbolism, but restored only to the powers which the revolution of 1640 had left it. The church was fenced about with new laws against dissent, or rather against various practices of conscientious dissenters. The law-courts resumed their sittings, to remain unreformed for 200 years. The democratic movement ended. Nothing was done to remedy the grievances of the poor, and, whatever improvement there may have been in the price of bread, it is surprising that there was little popular discontent.[7] Local riots and disturbances did not turn into rebellions. The leaders of the new opposition demanded toleration and parliamentary government; in London they used the mob and finally they chose the path of revolution. The one feeble rebellion, that of Monmouth in 1685, came after long preparation from above. The final outcome was the Revolution of 1688, a movement led by noblemen and not resisted by anyone on grounds of class-interest. By a network of compromises it established such a degree of freedom in each compartment of the national life as would enable the political machine to work harmoniously until a century later, when the Industrial Revolution subverted the social bases of politics.

One of the strange features of the civil war is that in it there fought not only proud, selfish and violent men, but men to whom the restraints of discussion had become second nature. Are we to regard it as an abandonment of the habit of discussion, or was it a culmination, or Nemesis, the inevitable result of trying to apply discussion to contentions which it could only exasperate? Neither answer would be completely satisfactory without something of the other. Before, during and after the war there was unprecedented activity in political discussion both by word of mouth and in writing. There were authors and pamphleteers who showed every literary merit from depth of thought to perfection of phrase. With very few exceptions they did not invent new ideas but brought the best ancient and modern thought to bear on the day-to-day emergencies of the time. But the breakdown of the constitution brought it about that much of what they wrote could not direct opinion into channels of effective action, and could only inflame the opposing passions. Discussion lost touch with responsibility.

Added together those liberties which were established as the outcome of the seventeenth-century struggles seem to give something at least generically like the modern liberal state. Such a state is conceived of as offering freedom to individuals and to voluntary combinations of individuals, interfering only to prevent them from interfering with one another. It guarantees the individual's own disposal of his person, his property, his thoughts and words, his conscience. In addition to this immunity it gives him equality with his fellows before the law. It gives him a share as an elector in choosing or even in controlling those who are set in authority over him, so that, granted a certain degree of civic sense in accepting the decisions of the majority, such a state is governed by consent. It relies on free competition to attain the maximum economic returns, and on voluntary charity to correct inequalities in the distribution of wealth. There has never been a state of which all these things were true, but some states have approximated to this type, and the type has been an operative ideal, setting goals for action in many times and places. There have also been other ideals opposed to it, protectionist ideals of diverse kinds, in which individual liberty was expressly related to notions of common social interest and material welfare.

The first classic of the liberal idealists was John Locke's *Second Essay on Civil Government*, which was written in earlier years and published immediately after the revolution of 1688 'to justify to the world the people of England'. It justified the step by which they had freed their elected legislature from the control of the executive, and had ended the arbitrary interference of that executive with persons and property and with the regular operation of the law. In another work, the

Letters on Toleration, Locke defended freedom of worship as it was conceded in England. There were limits and exceptions to this freedom of worship, and neither the representative government nor the freedom of property defended by Locke was democratic. For him 'the people of England' were the enfranchised minority, and property was in fact what a man owned under the laws which that minority made. His doctrine should be classed as aristocratic liberalism; it rejected the claims of the monarchy to interrupt the due course of law and legislation either for its own ends or on behalf of its subjects. Nor did it imply the full theory of economic liberalism as that was to develop about a century later. Locke himself as an administrator and pamphleteer worked within the general assumptions of protectionism.

Locke's England and his writings may easily seem closer to fully-developed liberalism than they really were. The state left individuals and associations to their own devices partly because in those days it was a smaller and weaker organization than it has since grown to be even in the most liberal states. The volume of legislation grew and the machinery of central government did increase in size, especially with the need for military and naval organization, but there was no fundamental change. Even the organization for war involved little direct contact with the individual inhabitants: the billeting officer was not allowed to requisition rooms in private houses; there was no national register of men liable for service in the militia or the army, and attempts to register all seamen in imitation of the French were unsuccessful. Even in France and Brandenburg-Prussia the pressure of the state on society was still light; but in England it was lighter than even in Holland where, at any rate, there was something better in the way of police. Much work of an executive nature was done by the local government authorities, especially by the extra-legal oligarchy of justices of the peace. They were appointed by the Crown, and the Crown continued in Queen Anne's time occasionally to dismiss those of them who were politically open to objection. They were addressed by the justices of assize, whose charges were expressions of government policy. At uncertain intervals they received orders from a secretary of state. But they were substantially independent. As there were no regional interests, even in Wales and the North, which could possibly embarrass the central authorities, there was no need for any effective central authority except that of parliament.

Freedom from regulation by central administrative authorities was thus not won in a continuing struggle. It arose from the tolerably satisfactory working of the local institutions. A second great article of the system, which had been a revolutionary demand, came about in practice because it served the convenience of everyone concerned. This was the assembling of a parliament in every year. In order to carry on their wars King William and Queen Anne needed a parliamentary grant of money every year, and they could only obtain such grants in the form of earmarked allocations for specified purposes, subject to businesslike provisions for raising taxation and controlling expenditure. 'The fact that England was free from invasion during a period which was on the whole a period of commercial growth and prosperity, coupled with the fact that the English kings desired to pursue an aggressive and therefore an expensive foreign policy, rendered possible a process of bargaining which necessarily resulted in acquisition and consolidation of the powers of Parliament.'[8] Except for the word 'aggressive' this sentence, which was written about the fifteenth century, is equally true of this period.

At first it seemed possible that parliament might wish to undertake the direct control of the war and of other important spheres of executive action. In 1689 the commons criticized the administrative preparations for the Irish campaign of the next year, and the king invited them to nominate up to seven persons whom he could commission 'to take care' of them. After considerable debate, they declined.[9] In 1691, however, there was a plan to make a surprise attack on the prerogative by giving direct control of the war to a committee.[10] In 1696, by creating the board of trade and plantations the government frustrated a scheme for parliamentary administration in this sphere. In 1689 commissioners for wool were appointed by an Act of Parliament with power to seize ships which engaged in smuggling it. All the powers of the commission were concurrent with those of other authorities. Their servants seized two French ships which had passed the customs, thus causing an embarrassing international incident. In 1701 the commission lapsed. From 1700 to 1702 the commissioners for the resumption of grants in Ireland carried out very large administrative operations and did so as agents of the English parliament. But it did not require the experience of these bodies to prove that the legislature would do better not to take executive work into its own hands.

The solution which has lasted in principle down to the present day was not the separation of the legislative and executive powers but what was known in Canada, in the crisis of the eighteen-thirties, as responsible government. Its shape was settled by a series of rapid adjustments which were not completed until 1707, when a limit was set to the power of ministers to control the members of the house of commons by giving them paid employment. That was the year of the union with Scotland, a triumph of common sense and public spirit, and that although it was not invulnerable to legal cavil. The constitutional settlement as a whole had similar defects. It was full of inconsistencies. There were dormant powers which might be roused and established practices which might be challenged. The sovereign retained a veto on legislation which has never been exercised since 1708, an unlimited power of creating peers which gave no trouble until 1832, the sole command of the armed forces, and an incompletely defined prerogative. The judges were appointed by the executive, and could be dismissed by the legislature, which has never done it. The upper house could throw out a supply bill, and never did so until 1909. And so on. All through the eighteenth century the revolution settlement held together. It survived severe strains and dangerous crises at home and abroad, and it guaranteed the liberties which made national co-operation possible.

The constitutional settlement was the guarantee, but its value depended on the value of that which it guaranteed, namely freedom in ways of life and thought. Theoretically perhaps all men might live and think alike, and yet do so freely; but in ordinary life we doubt whether they are free if no alternative choice is open to them. Variety is always favourable to freedom and often necessary to it. In England the strongest of the forces maintaining variety in styles of life was religion, and it was the strongest because it inspired not only individual consciences but bodies of like-minded men.

After the Restoration of Charles II freedom was restricted in those spheres from which a revival of revolutionary disturbance was feared, and after the Revolution of 1688 the same treatment was meted out to the supposed lurking-places of Jacobite reaction. This meant that there were new laws against the Roman Catholics in addition to the old, and there were still both the old and the recent laws against the Protestant dissenters. The long written discussion for and against freedom of opinion had not yet reached an agreed conclusion. The licensing of the press was administered harshly in the early years of Charles II, and not without vigilance until it was dropped in

1695.[11] Even then it was only outside the political sphere that authors, printers, and publishers enjoyed substantial liberty. The law of seditious libel and the special law against libelling peers of the realm were still severe.[12] Some of the points on which conviction or acquittal may turn are now decided by juries, but were decided then by judges. By an Act of 1712 every newspaper had to carry a stamp costing 1*d.*, and every pamphlet of more than half a sheet had to pay a duty of 2*s.* a sheet. Two years later the tory house of commons expelled the whig journalist Steele for his party writings, and until that year, the last year of Queen Anne, the bare possibility of an opposition press was in danger.

The foundation of all the later growth of freedom was laid when the Toleration Act of 1689 granted freedom of conscience and, with exceptions, freedom of worship. Henceforth there could be no body resembling an inquisition or using an inquisitorial procedure. In spite of the new penal laws the Revolution is held by some authorities to have rendered the lot of the Roman Catholics better than it had been in the time of Charles II; but this view seems to exaggerate the gap between the letter of the law and its enforcement. They were excluded from public office, from commissioned rank in the army and navy, and from many activities in the professions. Freedom of conscience was insufficient for them because they could not practise their sacramental religion without priests. In 1700 priests were made liable to life imprisonment for saying Mass, and, though this was a dead letter, they were unable to carry on their work without precautions and concealments. Roman Catholic landowners were nominally or actually under weighty disabilities. As prejudice declined the judges interpreted the laws as favourably to the papists as was possible; but for about a century after the Revolution they were in a condition of discouragement and decline.

Protestant nonconformists were treated much better. Their worship became lawful so long as they did not meet behind closed doors, and penalties were prescribed for any who should disturb it. In 1698 an Act against blasphemy included penalties for denying Christian doctrine, and these threatened Unitarianism, a tendency which accorded well with some of the characteristic ideas of the time, and was spreading into some of the nonconformist bodies. But this Act too had little effect. It was almost true by 1714 that all forms of religious belief were permitted, including that of the Jews, who had been quietly accepted, to the marked advantage of the country, since the Cromwellian protectorate.

So far the position in England was not very different from that in Holland, indeed in one respect it may have been rather better. In Holland the federal character of the republic made it comparatively easy to set up this freedom of worship without civil rights, and also the freedom of the press, which flourished there much earlier and more securely than in England. If one province had tightened or even enforced its laws against Roman Catholics and sectaries, the others would have seen their advantage in opening their doors to refugees.[13] To be tolerated is something; it is another and a different thing to stay where you are and to be as you are with an equal and perfect right. Toleration may be due to mere indifference, which is not far removed from contempt. It may be conferred for a purpose or conceded at a price. It may breed resentment, and it may close the minds of the two parties to mutual understanding. The chances are against a wholesome relationship between the authorities and those whom they tolerate. In England toleration owed less than in Holland to extraneous circumstances and more to the spirit of tolerance, which some notable royalist divines and laymen had advocated even in the days of Charles I. It gradually spread among the ruling circles in church and state, and sometimes it reached the level at which tolerance is not only reconcilable with religious conviction but integrated with it.

In one respect, however, the Dutch treated differences of opinion more liberally than the English, in the very important respect of academic freedom. No thorough-going doctrine of academic freedom had indeed as yet been formulated. In no country did either the government or the authorities in the universities disclaim responsibility for the orthodoxy of university teaching. In the early eighteenth century some of the teachers in some German universities began to claim freedom to teach as they thought. The Dutch universities had not reached this position, but in practice they enjoyed a comparable liberty. Federation favoured diversity in the universities as in religion; there were four of them, and their rivalries mitigated the pressure for conformity. When the governments of the provinces interfered, their chief or sole purpose was to damp down the acrimony of academic disputes. This was one of the many reasons which enabled the Dutch universities to cater for some of the educational needs of all protestant Europe.

Apart from some notable but occasional visitors from a distance, the two English universities served only English needs. It is indeed true that here also, except during the ill-fated alliance of King Charles I and Archbishop Laud, the government seldom interfered with the day-to-day affairs of the universities except in the interests of peace and decorum; but after the Restoration they were virtually closed to all except members of the Church of England, and the granting of toleration made no difference to this. Only Anglicans could take degrees, and except in the not very important faculties of law and medicine, teaching and study were in the hands of clergymen. It was intended that institutional education for positions of responsibility should not be accessible to the nonconformists. Furthermore, the right to teach in a school depended on a licence from a bishop. When Charles II tried to introduce toleration by prerogative some of the nonconformists ventured to open schools of their own, and in William III's time there was a judicial decision which set limits to the control of the bishops. The continuous history of nonconformist education dates from that time; but during the reaction under Queen Anne a new Act forbade any nonconformist to keep a school. This was the last of the attempts to extinguish dissent in all walks of life except the humblest. Like the other reactionary legislation of the time it was soon ignored, though not repealed, but even without it nonconformists were shut out from the best educational opportunities until far on in the reign of Queen Victoria.

This was so much a primary fact of English history in the eighteenth and nineteenth centuries that it is impossible here and now to estimate its effects, ramifying throughout the national life. We are concerned only with its place in the history of freedom. It retarded and hampered the freedom of thought in Oxford and Cambridge. They were not so inactive as is commonly supposed; within their permitted limits they assimilated the best of contemporary thought; but they were largely unaware of the existence among the nonconformists of a second stream of English civilization, complementary to their own, creative, in spite of its disparity of status, and full of various promise.

The nonconformists were a minority. It is hard to remember that in 1700 they probably did not number more than about a tenth of the population. It is hard because a century later a large accession of reinforcements or allies, the Methodists, greatly changed their numerical position. They were divided among themselves. There were many sects besides the three 'persuasions' which maintained a common representation for official dealings with the government while they disagreed energetically about theology and church practices. But the historic influence of a minority which is divided from the majority by conviction does not depend on its numbers. The English protestant dissenters were the custodians of some elements of religion which could not find scope in the Church of England. Not all of them were ultra-protestant elements: in the position of the laity and especially of women some of the sects provided for needs which the Roman church understood, and the same may be said of some of their theological ideas. And the nonconformists had not only their beliefs but also their tradition. They looked back on the history of 'the good old cause', the rise and fall of Puritanism, and no one could share with them their half-avowed pride and regrets. In literature, in scholarship, even in architecture, they developed their tradition. Historians have not done justice to it.

This second stream of English culture contributed from the beginning to the main stream, the established culture of the majority who enjoyed the unqualified countenance of the law and of the ruling elements. Bunyan's *Pilgrim's Progress* was dreamed in prison, but it was read in every kind of home. Milton took his rightful place as one of the greatest in the great line of national poets. Isaac Watts, already famous in Queen Anne's reign as a writer of hymns, was in due time to be honoured with a monument in the cloister of Westminster Abbey, not in the abbey church itself, but on the premises. From these men and from many lesser writers and teachers there was a steady flow of knowledge and ideas into the greater stream. Isaac Watts was educated at one of the academies which the nonconformists set up when they were compelled intellectually to shift for themselves. Another had two pupils of whom one, Thomas Secker, became archbishop of Canterbury, and the other, Joseph Butler, became the greatest of Anglican theologians. Neither of them went over to the Church of England empty-handed.

The nonconformists could not escape all the conflicts between the different requirements of freedom. In some ways their academies could not equal the standards of the universities; in others, since they decided their own curriculum, they were pioneers of eighteenth-century thought. But within their own walls there were limits to their tolerance and comprehension. There was a point beyond which they would not dilute the dissident quality of their inheritance. For their own people and from their own point of view that was, of course, the justification of their being; but it made them impermeable to some influences from outside, and in particular to those from the universities and the established church. It engendered, in the religious and intellectual sphere, a narrowing parallel to the self-imposed narrowing of the establishment. It restricted their sympathies as well as their intellectual range, even when they had sympathy and understanding for fields which were invisible to the conventional view of the universities.

Thus the long estrangement between the two traditions spelt both loss and gain for each of them, and it was only very slowly, through mutual knowledge and respect, that each acquired a deeper appreciation of its own belief as an alternative freely preferred. But in the last decades of Stuart England such insight was already beginning to germinate. It is no mere paradox to maintain that not least among the services of the nonconformist minority, and of each lesser minority within it, to the nation as a whole and even to the majorities from which they dissented, was the service they rendered in their own day and generation by persisting in their separateness and freedom.

NOTES

1 The text is given with slight differences by J. Rushworth, *Historical Collections*, iv (1692), 453, and in part by Clarendon, who drafted it, in his *History of the Great Rebellion*, ed. W. D. Macray (1888), i. 437.

2 S. R. Gardiner, *History of the Great Civil War* (ed. of 1893), iv. 320. The expression 'liberty and freedom' is still sometimes used, but, although they are customarily used in different contexts, there seems never to have been any difference of meaning between 'liberty' and 'freedom'. It does not seem possible to translate them differently into any other language.

3 *Clarke Papers*, ed. C. H. Firth, i (1891), 209, 277.

4 R. Lennard, *Rural England, 1086–1135* (1959), p. 62.

5 See the memorable lecture of Professor Wallace Notestein, 'The Winning of the Initiative by the House of Commons', in *Proceedings of the British Academy*, xi (1924).

6 P. Laslett, 'The Gentry of Kent in 1640', in *Cambridge Historical Journal*, ix (1948), 148 ff.; M. H. Curtis, *Oxford and Cambridge in Transition* (1959), cs. iii, v, x.

7 See M. Beloff, *Public Order and Popular Disturbances, 1660–1714* (1938).

8 Sir William Holdsworth, *History of English Law*, ii (3rd ed., 1923), 430. For a detailed account of the bargaining in and before this time

see D. Ogg, *England in the Reign of Charles II* (2nd ed. 1955), ii. c. xiii, and *England in the Reigns of James II and William III* (1955), c. xvii.

9 W. Cobbett, *Parliamentary History*, v (1809), 467–72.

10 Sir Robert Howard to William III, 31 July 1691, in Sir John Dalrymple, *Memoirs of Great Britain and Ireland* (1790), iii. 188.

11 See J. Walker, 'The Censorship of the Press during the Reign of Charles II', in *History*, xxxv (1950), 219 ff.

12 For the results in a special department of literature see H. Macdonald, 'The Law and Defamatory Biographies in the Seventeenth Century', in *Review of English Studies*, xx (1944), 177 ff.

13 This, the view of Robert Fruin in his later years, is expressed in an article of 1865 reprinted in his *Verspreide geschriften*, i (1900), 39 ff. It is disputed by J. W. Smit, *Fruin en de partijen tijdens de republiek* (1958), pp. 157–8, who, however, appears to convict Fruin of underestimating the services of the regents to freedom, not of being wrong in what he positively says. The penetrating and suggestive book of Dr. H. E. Enno van Gelder, *Vrijheid en onvrijheid in de republiek*, i (1947), *van 1572 tot 1619*, should, when completed, provide a basis for comparisons between Dutch and British freedom.

Printed in Great Britain by
The Camelot Press Ltd., London and Southampton